KU-346-282

MORAY COUNCIL LIBRARIES & INFO.SERVICES	
2O 2O 82 92	
Askews	
305.891497	

Weather worn and battle torn — Phie Price

Acknowledgements

I was fortunate to be able to gather a collection of my own photographs along with others belonging to relatives and various other Gypsies who have trodden and rolled the same road as myself.

The photographs have been reproduced to their best from originals supplied, many of which are very old and have suffered from being frequently handled and in some cases not well stored.

I am indebted to all people who have assisted in making this book possible and I hope that all Gypsies, past, present and, I hope, future will look back and enjoy the visual record of the photographs produced. I also thank all the people who have copyright on pictures or text for permission to reproduce them.

I am particularly grateful to Derbyshire Gypsy Liaison Group and Siobhan Spencer and Bob Dawson for allowing me to use some of the material they have written.

Cover: Tuck oilette postcard dating from 1904.

Creddy Price, Old Casey Ivy's mam and Creddy's brother Ivor.

Foreword

My mam was Elizabeth Price and my dad Hope Price. My grandfather was Creddy Price who was a soldier in the 1st World War. There were 12 in my family but 3 or 4 died young. Only one of us was born in a hospital, that was why we called him Gypsy Boy. I was born in a wagon and my brother in a bow tent and we never saw a doctor when we needed to. Life was hard but life was good. I used to go out with my mam when she was hawking when I was five years old. I can remember when we used to go around and they wouldn't give you a biscuit or a bit of bread or anything. My mam used to beg them to give us a bit of bread — nothing. They used to shut the door on my mam. That was how hard life always was.

Then, a boy was always taught to learn to fight. A girl was taught to carry a basket straight away. She'd go out selling. I was wheeling and dealing at ten years old, buying and selling horses and at 14 I had my own business. I had a licence at 21. That was the way of the Gypsy. You had to learn how to survive. You didn't depend upon social or anything like that. If you didn't work you didn't get anything.

My old grandmother used to sit down and teach me Romanes. I didn't want to listen to her long. I didn't listen to her enough, It wasn't that I didn't want to understand, listening was enough. She could speak it like she was speaking English. She was one of the proper old Gypsies. She said that one day I'd regret not listening to this. Her mam was old Polly. She died when she was about 90 and she died when she was about 95 or 100 and her mam was old Emily Slender.

Nobody really knows where the Gypsy comes from. A lot of people say we come from India and I've heard others say we come from Romania. The first Gypsies landed in Scotland. Indians have a lot in common with the Gypsies. We speak the same language, have the same culture as them. We won't wash in the same dishes, we always use different bowls for everything. We believe a woman has to be right before we can marry her because the Bible says this and we believe in the law of decency. If you keep a young girl out until morning and she was a decent girl, you have to marry her — that's our law. When you brought her back next morning you made an arrangement to have a bit of a do and you were married, whether you liked it or not. A girl got married at a young age. My mam got married at 15. I've got a picture of my dad at 16 years of age just married with my mam. He had to build his own wagon. That was Gypsy life.

I've travelled everywhere, all over the country, but I like it best in Yorkshire and round here, Derbyshire, Nottinghamshire. I was born in Barnsley. It's home but it has all changed.

Since we have become Christians, things are different. And Gypsies have changed a lot. I got married again after seven years to please God, to be obedient to God and to do what the Bible says. God blessed the wedding at Canaan. Two of my boys are married to Gypsy girls. If you don't love the girl, a piece of paper isn't going to alter it. It doesn't really matter, because when a Gypsy man takes a woman, he loves her. I know there are different men, who'll swap and change, but a proper man will stick with his girl. It's a bully who changes his woman.

I've heard it said that the history of the Gypsies goes back a thousand years to Egypt and we belonged to a Pharaoh. The Pharaoh gave them twelve months and gave them a donkey and a camel apiece and said, "You can make it. Come back in twelve months." When they came back, he doubled everything they had and they were given their freedom. So then they went to all the corners of the world. But nobody really knows where they came from. They went to India about 800 years ago and they've been in England about 500 years. You get the name Gypsy from Egypt. Years ago we were slaves. We were sold to whoever bought us, the lord of the manor, and we bear their name. Whoever owned you, in twenty years time you were still their man. That's where the name Price comes from. When we first started coming over here, the first tribes landed in Scotland and Ireland and they were Kalderash or Sinti or whatever, but it is our slave name we live by. Gypsies in America were also sold as slaves, and they are called Prices or Lees. That's where we come from — slavery.

I think we're in the Bible. There is a woman there who was reading fortunes, telling people the future — Sarah I think. I think she was a Gypsy. That's going back two thousand years and God didn't condemn us then so why are we being condemned now? A lot of people think we're a lost tribe of Israel. We have a Jewish preacher and he can't deny it. Israel can't deny it either. But Israel won't recognise us and the reason is that if she did, they would have to stand proud and look after us.

I think what Mr. Howard said was prejudice. He doesn't understand what's going on. He was that desperate to win he didn't care how he did it. Things have been tougher since then. I've had firms who I've had work from for twenty years who are now saying, "Gypsies are doing this, Gypsies are doing that". Any other time they would have just accepted me as a Gypsy but now it has started some hatred against us. If that man takes our rights we're finished. *(During the 2005 election, Michael Howard, leader of the Conservative Party, made derogatory remarks about Travellers. There were various incidents, including two involving separate branches of the Price family who had windows smashed and one trailer burned out respectively — Ed).* My children have all left school now, so it hasn't affected them.

I can remember the wagons, and the old Blue Bird caravans. When we

8

were in wagons, the small children slept in bed with their parents. Bigger ones slept underneath the bed, and the bigger ones still outside under the wagon with a canvas sheet round. It made you very hard — you had to be — getting up at 6am for a wash in cold water.

Moving from wagons into motorised trailers was hard because the men had to learn the new ways. There are changes for the better and changes for the worse. People say they were the good old days, but how can they have been the good times when we never had bread to eat? People think it was the romantic stuff but it was really hard. Now things can get very hard but when you look back it was nothing because you're still here. You took everything the world had to give to you — the world chucked everything against Gypsies, but we're still here. It made no difference. Everything they chucked at us but we still survived.

They tried to kill us in the Holocaust, they tried to kill us in Spain, they tried to kill us in France. In one part of Spain they used to hang a Gypsy each morning because they thought it was lucky to hang a Gypsy but there are still Gypsies in Spain. If you shot or killed a Gypsy there was a reward from the king because you had done good. There were times when you were boiling a pot on an outside fire and the *gorjers* would check whether you were boiling babies which had been stolen, so they had the right to come and tip the pot over and check what was in it, and that's why the pot had to be boiled in the open. That's the word that has been passed down to us, and I don't know if it is true.

We love children and we will look after them. When I was first married, I went to a chip shop and there was a woman who had a baby on the counter and it was beautiful. She said, "I don't want it, I don't want the rubbish. Take it." Just like an animal — "Take it". She gave me it. An old granny came out screaming, "You can't take it, just because she can't rear it." I gave the child to the old woman. But if the child had gone with me, it would have been reared really well. We adopt children others don't want. Asian girls, Black boys, whatever. I have a cousin who has adopted a Chinese baby. She grew up and she has four or five children of her own and she married a Gypsy boy and she is a Gypsy. There are two or three black girls who I class as my cousins because they have been reared with us as Gypsies and they have babies of their own. People don't see that side of us.

When my children were at school, it was always a battle. From day one there was fighting but they looked after themselves. One boy, who was black, called one of my boys names because he was a Gypsy so my boy gave him a hiding. Then his mother came out and hit my boy. Then my wife went down and threatened her. She said we were prejudiced because my wife had threatened a black boy. So where does the law stand? By the way, my 9 year old grandson is a kick boxing champion and lots of Romany boys go in for boxing.

I've never been to school in my life. I never had the chance because when I was little we used to be on the road at 6 o'clock in the morning because the police had a routine. They used to rip you off 6 in the morning. There was one council man in Wolverhampton used to get you off at 5 because he used to like to see the women being got out of bed. He was a pervert and he got done for it. I can remember us being ripped off the side of the road because we weren't allowed near the road because it was a main road and made to move on at 7 o'clock at night — now where are you going to go at that time? Even four years ago when I was in Manchester at 11 or 12 o'clock at night the *gorjers* were breaking you up and you had to move. I had a very good friend in the police but when it came to push he was just like the rest.

My dad said to never trust the police when they were talking and I never trust a policeman. When a policeman comes to shout and tell you what to do then you know where you stand, but a sweet-talking man you can never trust. A Gypsy never trusts anybody. The only way a Gypsy survives is looking after their own and their own family but they are losing a lot of their culture because they've shared their Romany speech. Nearly every *gorjer* knows it.

Our Romani isn't that of the Kaldersash. I heard of an academic, a very clever man, who said that Romanus wasn't spoken at all in Britain and it made me very angry. The way the Gypsies are changing, I don't think there will be any more Gypsies on the road and that's what this book is for. It's something to look back on and know what Gypsy life was about. It's like the Native American Indians. They can look back on the past and say, "My Great Grandfather was a Cherokee" or whoever. One of the French Gypsy boys married an American Indian. They have beautiful children. Their people are taught like the Gypsy young men are taught. My dad used to tuck me up and say, "You can't be a *gorjer* boy, you're not a *gorjer* boy.

I've been buying and selling horses since I was six years old. I can handle any horse. It's something you work to, I've been up and down so many times with horses. I've tied ropes to my hand to hold a horse, and they burned, and you had to handle him. I've seen my brother kicked out of a horse box one day by a stallion and he was knocked spark out. We had the job then of getting the stallion. That's the way of life. I've always had horses.

To earn a living, I've done scrap, trees, tarmac, plastering — you name it, I've done it. But I don't steal, I don't rob. A true Gypsy doesn't steal, everyone who knows Gypsies knows that and lots of people say we do, but we don't need to. A Gypsy man can get his living anywhere in the world whatever way he can get his living. Every Gypsy man carries a bone handled penknife like a Native American Indian. Gypsies and Indians have a lot in common. It's like a religion for both of us. It's like the tool of my trade. I can make flowers or pegs, shave a hedgehog. It used to be the most important thing. A Gypsy wagon was made with a knife.

We didn't have a television. In those days it was warmth and food. We'd walk seven or eight miles just to find a rabbit and if you found a couple of hedgehogs it was a bonus. You'd go and get a few potatoes out of a field because the corner of a field is made for the Travellers and by law you can't touch the rest of the field so you'd go into a corner of the field and you could pick what you wanted to make a bit of dinner.

I'm proud of being a Gypsy. You are what you are. A black man can't be ashamed for being black. God made us Gypsies but we're the most hated people in the world. Nobody likes us, I don't care wherever you go to, there's no love for the Gypsy. All the Gypsy has done is try to survive. That's all we've done — live day to day, and if a Gypsy can get the best he'll have the best but we aren't allowed to do this. One man in Birmingham bought a house like a *gorjer* man and did it as he wanted it. Now people are complaining because it's too posh for the area. In the middle of a town, one of our lads got a site passed. Someone has taken the planning inspector to court who passed the site because he said he had no right to pass the plans for the site. The judge said it was nothing to do with them, it was his problem, but how can you take a judge to court?

I met my wife at Appleby. She was 21 and I was 20. A year before that my aunt read my fortune in the cards. She told me exactly who I was going to marry. My wife had her fortune told, and she was told she'd meet a man with a good heart. We had never seen each other before but it happened like the fortune tellers had said. I remember years ago among the old people, my father would say, "Don't *chinger* (argue with) her, she's a *chivihaun*," and that's a woman who puts a curse on you. So we always had respect for old people, though Gypsies always have respect for old people anyway. We look after old people. My children and all their children learn to respect older people.

About fortune telling, years ago there was an old woman who sold her soul to the devil and when she died and was in her coffin, she had two horns growing from her head. Years ago, the Gypsies used to mix the Lord God and the devil because we were no better friend in the world to the devil. He could convince you black was white. A Gypsy used to be a professional conman, he could convince you — it was in his best interests. There was a time when a five year old could read someone's fortune — I've had mine read a few times — because they're taught. In a Gypsy life a child is taught to read fortunes, to look after children, and the man's the man. He's the one who has to keep things going and to keep things right. In the past they were funny days. My wife would tell you that her dad, when her mother used to go out, if she came back with no shopping she'd get a good hiding and she'd be made to sleep in the motor. If he didn't get his beer money and his shopping that's what would happen. I've seen my dad do that to my mam. How could that be the good old days? These days are the best days of your life. Gypsy men are driving about in cars and years ago the closest thing you got to it was a bike.

Creddy Price was a quiet man but when he was in the pub he was a blackguard. He could fight. But his brother was the opposite. He fought for a living. Linchum Smith used to tell me about it. In the pub, Creddy was a hard man but Chasey wasn't because he had no need to do it. Take Nighty Lee. When he was on the ground, he was Nighty Lee and a nice man, an old gentleman and everyone loved him. When he was in the drink, he was Nighty Scamp. He used to ask people to keep an eye on his meal while it was cooking and he'd go to the pub, When he came back, you'd have cooked his food for him. I've watched him making pegs for hours and hours.

Years ago there was a bad man who was a fighting man and my wife's great uncle. He went to the pub and at the bar he had a couple of pints. A man sat there playing cards and asked him to play cards with him. He said he had no money, but the man said, 'Look in your pocket' and there in his pocket was a handful of money. Whilst he was playing cards, he dropped one and when he picked it up he saw that the other player had a cloven foot. He had always said he would fight the very devil himself. He set off running for his tent, home, but when he got there, about two miles away, there was the man sitting on a fence waiting, and he said, "Now what about this fight you've been on about for a long time," so the two of them had a fight and the devil gave him a hiding. The devil ripped his tent to bits. But he became a good man after that. That happened for real, because it's been passed on amongst our people for years.

A lot of things happened in those days. The old Gypsy men were hard. If my grandfather had a colt foal he would kill it because it was no good, but a mare foal he would keep. In the winter, there was no way you could keep two colts so you kept the one which would be of use later. And if they had a grudge against someone, they'd go miles, they wouldn't care if it was a hundred miles to fight someone and then afterwards they'd have a few pints and shake hands and that was it. For Gypsy men, fighting was their life. One reason was that we used to travel Wales. We used to fight the coal miners, and they were hard men. If you beat them, you were the best man in Wales, I had a great uncle, Creddy Price's brother Chasey

Price who died when he was either 37 or 47, I forget which, but he was a young man. He was an undefeated bare fist fighter amongst the boys, so they say now. He was hit over the head with a bottle and that gave him cancer and that's what killed him. There were a lot of great men amongst them. I had two uncles — my grandfather's step brothers — who died in WW2. They were mule soldiers in the Burmese jungle, taking ammunition out. The one not a sergeant used to get a bit of stick in the army because his brother was a sergeant. When they used to come home on leave they used to take their shirts off and they were Gypsy men again. Both were killed in Burma. When there's war, the Gypsy boys will fight. In the first Iraq war, many Gypsy boys from Evesham volunteered for the army and signed up. People don't know about or understand this.

Gypsy people and Irish Traveller people have learned to live with one another. We used to be scared of each other but these days we're reared together and we aren't scared any more. We have learned to live with each other. It's a cultural thing . We're aware of differences between ourselves and Irish Travellers or *Gorjers*. In the WW1, it must have been, the army police came to get a Gypsy man for the army. He was 18 and just married and in those days they could do that. He told his wife to hitch up and move, and about two miles down the road he rejoined her. He'd given four MPs a good hiding and escaped. They never did catch him and so he survived the war.

My dad used to say that to be a *rai* — a gentleman — it spoke for itself. Money spoke for itself. If you had a brand new caravan, a new car, a new lorry, you had it and there was the sign of your money. It didn't mean anything in the bank. My father used to say that if you hadn't got it, you didn't show it.

Fortune telling was a way of giving people advice. When our women went up and down hawking, people could talk to them and they gave them advice because they had a lot of experience and understood a lot of things. Some of the preachers now say we can't tell fortunes and we can't even have cooking pots outside because of the connection between the devil and witches and pots. Some say we can't even talk about the past because of the old ways of the Gypsies. Gypsies survived by word of mouth. They talked to each other and they knew each other by what they said. Now that secret has been allowed to come out and people have learned a lot about who we are. But we should keep our culture.

The born again Christian movement has been going amongst Gypsies now for 20 years. But you can't change a lifetime in 20 years. Those preachers who told Gypsies that as Christians they couldn't do this or that had never lived that way. How can they tell me how to live my life? I can't tell them how to live theirs.

At the conventions they'll have a cafe and a shop but if you try and sell a few clothes, it's against God. There are preachers who sell things, motors and such like, but say you can't. How can one be wrong and one be right? They say don't sign on the dole, but some people genuinely need it — not everyone can afford a trailer to live in. It's not an easy life for us.

Emily Lee (Harry's wife) and Jerald Price (wife of Hope)

Old Polly Price, Polly's daughter Tom Bon, Polly's daughter in law Star Price and Emily Lee (Big Harry Lee's wife)

Left, Linchum and Lucy Smith on their wedding day. Right, Linchum Smith

Emily Lee, Lucy Lee, Rina Lee and sister Beryl Lee

Inside wagon — Big Beryl, John and Creddy; on the ground, Lola, Pearl and Dancer Lee

Crimea Price, Billy Price and Harry (John Henry) Lee

Top — Fred Price's family;
bottom — Granny Lucy

Top — Hope Price with friends;
bottom — Gypsy encampment

Clockwise from top — Merry Lee (Big Harry Lee's sister) and Tom Bon Price; Milenda Price with daughter Lucky Price; Fred Price and wife Florrie with children Kevin, Righteous, Sister and Rellie.

Clockwise from top — Granny Lucy; Tenny Smith (Hope Price's granddad) in Burma, WW2; Crimea Price, Naily Lee, Billy Price and Davon Price

Mushy and Ophie Lee, the latter being the father of Clifford Lee

The Romany People

The Romany people have lived in England, Wales and Scotland for over 500 years and the Irish Traveller community about 150 years. It is quite difficult to understand and appreciate a different culture if one does not have enough information on that culture. Correct information diminishes prejudice.

Most *Gorjers* (non Gypsy) people do not know much about the Romany culture although they have lived in England for centuries. Amongst Irish Traveller families, you may hear the words buffer or countryman instead of *Gorjer* which means someone who is not Romany. Over the years the word has been mistakenly used to refer to people who do not travel.

It is often difficult for us to accept people who behave differently, who do not meet our norms. The strange and the unfamiliar often confuse us. We speak about equity but for many that means similarity.

On a daily basis, professional workers meet many different kinds of people. In order for them to be able to relate to their different clients and their cultures in a positive and correct fashion, they need accurate information concerning the background of their clients. It is important to see people as a part of their family, culture and the community they live in.

There have been attempts in the past at genocide against the Romany. One of the latest periods of persecutions occurred during the World War II. At least 600,000 Roma were killed in Hitler's gas chambers. The researchers' latest estimates of the number of Roma casualties run up to two million.

Beryl and Mary Lee

Crimea Price and friend

Silver, Helen, Lemme and Peggy Lee   Two Gypsy men at a fairground

Big Mary Lee

Oliver Lee, Warcop, Westmorland, 1911

Top — A Gypsy gathering;
bottom — Oliver Lee with Gypsy Lore Society members Fred Shaw, RAS
Macfie, George Hall and John Ferguson

Gypsy and gorjer gatherings

Top — Gypsy encampment; bottom — Gypsy ladies washing

Talaitha Cooper (nee Lee), wife of Wacker Cooper

Birth and Culture

Traditionally, Traveller fathers do not attend the birth of a baby. Many Traveller mothers will try to leave the hospital to go home with the baby as soon as possible after labour even though there are risks that relate to going home too early.

It was common earlier that when the mother and the child came from the hospital she was not able to do the household chores for a few weeks. She always had a "helper", either her husband other member of family or a friend who took care of the kitchen duties and looked after the mother. In many families this custom is still followed.

Babies are never breast-fed in front of strangers. Things to do with birth are not discussed in "mixed company" (men & women).

Togetherness of the family is important. If a relative is having hard times, then the rest of the family tries to help and provides support. These situations may include for example: financial difficulties, divorce, sickness and death. In a balanced Romany family the man and the woman do not compete against one another. The man is the head of the family and the woman is the heart of it. Both are important for the well being of the family. A man is appreciated according to how well he can support his family and a woman according to how well she manages the home and the children.

In the Romani community, the women are in a high standing. They create the atmosphere of the home and are fundamentally strong persons in a feminine way. Although Romani women still have many responsibilities they do not usually feel themselves oppressed. The question of equality between men and women is not important. The men are in the background when issues connected with the role and status of women are dealt with and vice versa.

On the other hand, it is important to notice that the differences in the roles of men and women can allow some men to discriminate and treat their families badly. This phenomenon is not due to the Romani/Traveller culture but usually it is due to the problems within the family.

The decreasing role of the men as influential persons in the family is visible in the modern development of the society and families. Traveller women have always had the right and the duty to work outside the home to provide for the family. Therefore it has always been easier for the women to re-educate themselves and to find their place in the labour market. In the near future special measures should be taken to prevent the Traveller men from marginalisation.

The elders and the children have always been special groups within the Romani culture in general. They play an important role in both women's and men's roles. Both genders are responsible for the well being of the elders and the children.

It is typical for all the members of the Romani community to take part in the upbringing of the children. Although it is seen as the women's duty to pass on the traditions, the fathers play an important role in their children's well being in relation to other Travellers

How much a child learns in school or how skilled and able he/she is, is not primarily important to Traveller parents. It is important for the child to have a safe and happy childhood. The Traveller children have a lot of knowledge of people and human nature from quite an early age. They receive teaching and wisdom from the adults and a child learns to live as a member of the community from birth.

The Traveller children have to face other people's negative attitudes early on in their life and because of that, the parents strive to give the sons and daughters strong roots so they can deal with the difficulties they may face.

Travellers have not placed their children in day-care until quite recently.

In today's world, it is the positive aspects of Gypsy culture that need to be pointed out — close family ties and traditional values. It is very easy to pick out health problems and relate them to the culture rather than to relate them to the fact that the majority do not want to accept the minority culture. We all need a safe base.

Julia, wife of Oliver Lee,
daughter of Bui Boswell,
with daughter Kenza (taken
Burton Lonsdale, 1916);

A Gypsy family

Mr. and Mrs Price and child

Creddy Price

Top — Linchum Smith and friends having a drink;
Bottom — Old Walton Lee, son Sandy and his daughter, Lucy Price,
Chassy Price and Charlotte

Clockwise from top left — Photo includes Ophie Price, Cocky Lee, Ivor, Willie Lee and La La.;
Below left: Ivy Lee; below right: Beryl, Winkie and Rita

Amongst the Lees and Prices on this photo are Punch Billy and his wife Emily, Ivy, Lucy, Lenny, La La, Cuddy, Harry, Sashy, Mary, Chassy and Embly Lee, and Righteous Price

Top — The funeral of the mother of old Paddy Lee;
bottom — the family of Creddy Price

Clockwise from top — The funeral of Creddy Price; Old Fatty Lee and son Nighty Lee; Old Star Price;

Elvie Buckley and grandchildren
Drue's Dad, Nighty Lee

Gypsy Work

In an agricultural society, the differences between the majority population and Travellers were not big. Education was not valued because the crafts were learned from father to son and mother to daughter. The difference in the level of education increased with industrialisation and progress.

Traditionally, Gypsy men worked in tasks associated with horse trading and horse handling, although some of course worked in other trades. During the summer time many made their living as handymen in agriculture. The women sold things door to door, hawking or knocking. The whole family took part in earning the living. The occupations required the families to move from one village to another and favoured private entrepreneurship.

Industrialisation made the traditional occupations of Travellers unprofitable and new occupations had to be found.

Some schemes for adult education have offered a chance to modernise the traditional skills to meet the modern needs but there is little joined up thinking across Great Britain as a whole and more could be done in some areas. The traditional occupations have laid a good basis for new occupations like horse trading for the selling of used cars, retailing commodities for starting a small business, the traditional women's skills for working as a dressmaker or a seamstress. The strongly expanded harness racing has provided a livelihood for some in various occupations relating to the raising and training of the horses.

Traditional Travellers both Romany and Irish, are reserved towards education since the school had been seen as one means to assimilate Travellers into the society of the majority. The attitude towards education has changed during the last few years to a positive direction regarding the fact that the majority would like to see the children go through primary school. There is not a big uptake on secondary level school, however early apprentice schemes seem to be popular with the traditional fairground community and may be picked up in the future by other Traditional Travellers.

*Top, Nighty Lee;
bottom, some of John and Rose Lee's 21
grandchildren.*

Left — Hope Price at Barnet Fair, 1982;
Right — Elizabeth Price at Barnet Fair, 1982

Top — Sam Price and his son John at Deeping Gate, 1964;
bottom — Carolina (Tomba, wife of Sam Price) at the wash tub with
daughters and pet fox

Left — Star Price and Jerald Price;
Right — Freedom Price and family

Clockwise from top — Hope Price; Lilly Buckley, wife of Needles Price; Old Opie Price, Shaun and Mary at Appleby Fair

Top — Peme Price, Star Price and family; Bottom — Lees: Ivy, Mary, Pearl, Dear, Poppy, Harry, Dancer and Beryl

Hope Price senior, Hope Price junior and Pretty Boy Price

Left — Old Thorny; right — Nin Lee

Chrissy and Maud Smith with children

Dolly and Georgie Smith

Lucy and Betty Price

Top — Lou May Evans and Nanna Evans;
bottom Mary, Debbie and Rosalind Lee

Clockwise from top left — Creddy Price, Old Zack Finney and family, Morren Finney, Bill Price

Top — Harry Lee, Reuben and Toffee;
bottom — Amanda Price (child), Elvie Buckley and old Katie Lee

Clockwise from top left — Gypsy children; Seph and Pompy Lee; Elvie Buckley and Pearl

Top — Mary Lee;
bottom — Tommy Lee and family

59

The History of the Price Family

The Journal of the Gypsy Lore Society claims that the first generation of Romany Prices were Henry Price and his wife Helen (or Ellen), nee Ingram, who travelled Shropshire and parts of Wales in the days of Queen Victoria. They are still regarded as Welsh Gypsies, no matter where they are found.

In fact, there were Romany Prices over 200 years before this, though Henry and Ellen's numerous children were the forebears of most of the modern day Prices. Henry and Ellen's children inclued Fighting Fred, who married Saiforella Wood; Bob, married Ellen Braddock; Siani who married William Smith; Dick who married a Welsh gel; Mary, who married Black Billy Wood and Posh Amos whose wife was Mary Ann Daly. They all had many children, many marrying Lees, Woods, Slenders and Smiths, whose names are still amongst today's Prices — Sampson, Gabriel, Arthur, Billy, Golias, Hope (Opie), Chasey, Creddy, Star, Naylus, Helen, Shushi, Crimea, Charlie, Amos, Darkis, Drui, Gerral, Perus, Seph and of course Fred.

Interestingly, recent DNA tests on Gypsies in various parts on the world show that Welsh Gypsies and Spanish Gypsies are very close genetically, showing common ancestries. Some traditions speak of Spanish Gypsies coming into Wales and a branch of those ending up in Derbyshire. Old Welsh Gypsies called themselves *The Kawlay* (meaning Black), the same word Spanish Gypsies call themselves by.

Top — Jim Price and family;
bottom — John Lee and family with Sam Price and baby

Clockwise from top left — Pompi and Rosie Lee; Rea and Beryl Price and friend; Beryl and Maureen Price and friend; Maureen Finney and Beryl Price

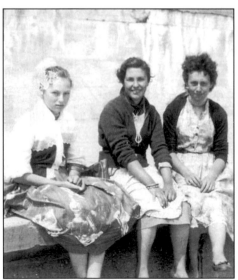

Top — Gypsy girls celebrating at the fair;
bottom — Rita and Bill Price at the fair

Top — Deer Price;
bottom — Harry Lee

Top — Brother Lee and his wife;
bottom — Michael Lee with brother and sister Mary and Rocky

Top — Izzy Price and family;
bottom — Harry Smith and family

Top — Barry Evans and Lincham Smith;
bottom — Old Peg Leg and Fred Lee, Bumper Price and family

Top — Izzy Price and family;
Bottom — Rita Lee, Thiga and Ninny

Top — Fred, Clifford and Shaun Lee;
bottom — Brothers Chrissy Boy, Doly and Harry Smith

Bricks and Mortar or a Site

Many traditional families have an aversion to bricks and mortar and become increasingly depressed when forced, (due in the main to the lack of sites and occasionally to ill health) to resort to living in a house.

There is an increasing suicide rate amongst Travellers because of this phenomenon.

Increasingly many families, because of the lack of sites, have sought their own provision by buying land to place their caravans on and to apply for planning permission for their own family because they want to remain living in a manner to which they were *born* to and did not choose. Over 90% of planning applications by families are turned down, as they fall into a catch 22 in the planning laws. As a result, many families are developing stress-related illnesses and nervous disorders

The increase of stress-related illness can be linked directly to the problems of a family not having a safe base to place their home.

For some Travellers living in a house, everyday life may have become easier, but new problems arise which an outsider finds difficult to understand and accept, without knowing the reasons behind the problems. For example, when a member of the family dies, some families will want to move as soon as possible. Assigning new housing will be necessary even if the person did not die in the residence, since some families will move out regardless. Also, in some cases, the customs and practises of the Romani families vary from one family to another.

Old Needles Price (known as Curly)

Left — Tom Lee and sisters and brother;
right — Maud Adeline Smith and great grandchildren

Old Darkiss's daughter Penny and Emily Price

Elvie and Pemmy Lee

Chasey and Linda Price

Top — Bill and Betsy Smith and children;
bottom — Sam, Jack and John Price

Top — Emberley Slender
bottom — Rosie, Bina and Salon;

Two pictures of Ivy Lee

Mary Lee and Muzelley

The Indian Link

Lots of people have tried to find out about how Gypsies came into being, and where they came from. Two of the best at finding the truth have been English Gypsy Professor Ian Hancock and *gorjer* Donald Kenrick.

The Romani language is an Indian dialect close to both Hindi and the old Indian language Sanskrit. This proves that Gypsies came originally from north-west India, mainly from the country now known as Pakistan. The Gypsy word *Rom/Romani/Romanes* is the same word as the Indian *Ramayana* and *Rama*. Other words in Romani prove that most spent a long time in Persia and in Greece before scattering through much of the world.

They were in India when the country had Himdusim as its religion, and they seem to have been part of the armies which defended India when the armies of Islam invaded. Many Gypsies were Rajput warriors, and others their families and camp followers. Some Gypsies may have left India before these times, but most were driven out by the Muslims when the country became Islamic. These first Gypsies were not only warriors but fine musicians, metal workers and animal doctors. Many of the old Romany customs date from those origins.

The earliest Gypsies in Britain almost certainly landed in Hull and in Cornwall, but others came south through Scotland. There may have been landings at other ports. Those earliest British Gypsies were small family bands who faced a very uncertain future.

Later, Gypsies from other places also arrived. Whilst it is certain that some of these were from Scandinavia and at least one band from Spain, there may have been others who came from other European countries.

Gypsies from other country continue to arrive from all over the place and to stay here and marry into British Gypsy families. Gypsy refugees from Yugoslavia, Czechoslovakia and Romania are amongst the most recent arrivals.

Top — Old Tombon and Old Mary;
bottom — Rita Lee

Old Mary Lee

Clockwise from top — Fred Lee; Harry Lee; Dancer Lee and children

83

Seph and Debbie Lee, wedding day

Pumpy and Puppy Lee, wedding day

85

Top — Green Grass country — Rita Lee, Creddy Price, and sons James and Chocky with actor Geoffrey Hughes.;
bottom — Kevin and Army Price

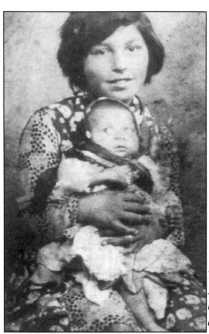

Top — Merry Lee and baby Rita Lee (Big Harry's daughter);
bottom — Young Opie (holding the baby) and some of the family — Appleby 1965

Left — Elvie Buckley and Dorothy Shaw;
right — Linchum Smith, Arnold Gray and Will Loveridge

The Romani Language

Romani is a member of the Indo-Aryan branch of the Indo-European family of languages. Its basis is the old Indian cult language Sanskrit, from which also Hindi, Urdu, Marathi etc. have evolved. Romani and Hindi are sister languages though Romani separated from the Indo-Aryan branch over a thousand years ago. In many ways it is older fashioned than the modern day Hindi. Romani is an internationally spoken language and according to various sources is spoken by approximately 40 million people in different continents and countries all over the world. In India alone there are over 20 million speakers of the Romani language. According to official sources, there are 8 million speakers of Romani in Europe and according to unofficial sources the number of the speakers of Romani is 12 million.

Over the course of time the Romani language has evolved into various dialects that have been influenced by the local languages. The researchers say that the basic vocabulary has stayed almost the same in various dialects. This is mainly due to the close connections between the Roma communities of different countries.

In England the dialect is known as Romanes. Due to the history of persecution many older Roma think that the less the outsiders know of their customs and language, the less they are able to hurt them. That is the reason for the unwillingness to teach the language to the outsiders. Earlier the language was adopted in natural settings. The diminished use of Romani means that the young know even less of the language and research highlighted this in the 1960s and 70s. Nowadays, the major changes in the Gypsy people's living conditions and the cultural turning point of great change have threatened the life and development of the Romani language.

The Irish Traveller language has a completely different route from Romany and it is not related in any way, but is it related to Gaelic. Over the years of contact and intermarriage between some Romani and Irish families, some words have crossed over from one group to another.

Top — Old Dick Boylam;
bottom — Harry Smith,
brother of Linchum, and
children

*Top — Tommy Taylor, Lucy Boswell, Darkis and Chinga Smith;
bottom — Ninny and Dawn*

Clockwise from top — Rosy Lee and Brother Lee;
Below — Lyncham Smith, Levam Lee and Tomy Lee;
Levam Lee and daughter Silver

Top — La La's children; bottom — Gypsy ladies getting ready for hawking

Bottom left — Elizabeth Price and family. Do you know the others?

Paddy, Frisco, and Seth Lee; Bob Braddock and friends

June and Rea

Jack and Creddy

Old Jack Taylor

Members of the Price family.

Left — Old Mary;
right — Data Price and grandchild

Recent Legislation

Over the years there has been a wide range of legislative measures, which have attempted to stop Romany people and Irish Travellers from leading a nomadic life and therefore from being. Measures date back as far as 1530 with the introduction of the *Egyptians Act*, which was a ban on the immigration of Gypsies and also expelled those already in England. More recent examples of legislation include:

The Highway and Byways Act 1959, which effectively criminalised the Travelling life overnight as families were not allowed to stop on the side of the road.

The Caravan Sites and Control of Development Act of 1960. Many families that had got to know farmers over the years were displaced by this act, since farmers could no longer allow them to stay on their land as they became eligible for fines if they technically ran a site without a valid site licence.

The 1968 Caravan Site Act led to the creation of sites by the local authority, but unfortunately many authorities flouted the law and did not build the sites that were needed.

The Criminal Justice and Public Order Act 1994 swept the *1968 Caravan Sites Act* away again criminalising this way of life. This act also gave the police increased powers including the right to impound vehicles if there were more than six. Guidelines issued to local authorities emphasised that before an eviction was carried out health, educational and social needs must be taken into account.

Top — Zack, Lucy, Leo, Mary and Permaline.;
bottom — Members of the Lee family

Mourners at the funeral of Star Price (Boggy's wife) — also following page.

Selina Lee with children Star and Tom

*Top — Hope, Pretty Boy and Elizabeth Price;
bottom — Hope and Gypsy Boy Price*

Top — Hope and Gypsy Boy Price;
bottom — Mary Lee

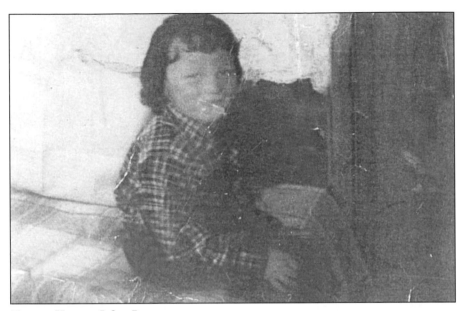

Top — Young John Lee;
bottom — Dancer, John and Fred Lee and others

Top — Members of the Price family;
bottom — Old Sally

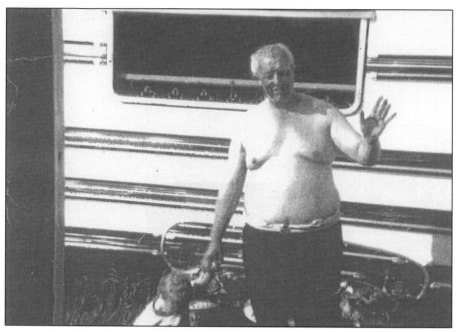

Top — Needles Price;
bottom — Lilly Buckley and Needles Price; Brother Lee (right)

110

Top — Pemmy Lee;
bottom — Cuddy Lee

Two poses of John Jones

Warrior Gypsies

The first Gypsies in Britain brought with them specialist knowledge of cannons. Since then, Gypsies have taken part in every single major British war, serving with distinction in both the army and navy. Britain's youngest VC winner was a Gypsy; another of the very young ones was a seaman; numerous others have won medals. One of the first members of the Special Operations Executive was a Gypsy who volunteered to stay behind in France after Dunkirk. Left with few resources but his own knowledge of nature and wild food, he was betrayed, and tortured and killed by the Gestapo.

The knowledge which Gypsies have of the countryside, animals and engineering have made them favourites for regiments like the Royal Engineers and the Chindits. The Black Watch has always recruited large numbers of Scotland's Travellers.

The Scamp family has always made its mark in both the Royal and Merchant Navies, whilst some Finneys lost their lives in the Zulu wars. Gypsies were amongst those who liberated Auschwitz though by a cruel twist of irony, every Gypsy in the camp had by then been murdered.

Gypsies are currently (2005) serving in Iraq and individuals found themselves in the fiercest fighting in the first Gulf War and the Falklands.

But few people outside the Gypsies themselves realise how much they have contributed to Britain's security.

Private John Cunningham, VC

A Soldier's Tale

Jamie was a proud tinker laddie who waved farewell to his parents as he set off to join his fellow Scots on the battlefields of France in the year of 1914, the time of the Great War.

Tinkers were treated like vermin in those days, but they still fought alongside many, and fell alongside them as well. A soldier once wrote: "generals', privates', dogs', and tinkers' blood mingles in the earth, an' nane can tell the difference." Notice the tinker is listed below a dog.

Two months before the end of the war, Jamie took a sniper's bullet to his left leg. The injury was not serious but his officer sent him home with the wounded, telling him to see a doctor when he got back.

The young man thought nothing of his injury as he made his long journey home to his people in the Highlands. In due course he eventually found them pearl-fishing in Caithness. His folks were over the moon that their laddie was returned to them, aye, and him with a medal. Sad to say, his leg wound was far more serious than he thought; poison had found its way into his bone. In those days this was fatal, and within a month Jamie, the brave tinker laddie who gave so much on the fields of France, died in his father's arms.

Relatives came for miles to mourn the brave laddie. While the men wandered back and forth discussing Jamie's heroics, the women prepared his body for the long rest.

Little balls of flax were placed in his ears and nostrils; this stopped evil spirits from entering his body and stealing away his soul. A small piece of ancient plaid embroidered with his family name was placed across his heart, ensuring a heavenly home for all the family, Lastly there was a gentle kiss from his parents before the body was wrapped in muslin cloth.

Within three days, over a hundred relatives had gathered for the journey to the secret burial ground. The sacred piece of land lay deep in the Highland glen, towered over on either side by high mountains, as if guarding their secret from the outside world. At the head of the little glen remnants of a once great Caledonian pine forest scatter themselves, bent with age, ravaged by rook and osprey nests, refusing to fall as if their very existence was a mark of Scotland herself.

REPRODUCED BY KIND PERMISSION FROM *JESSIE'S JOURNEY*, THE FIRST IN JESS SMITH'S THREE-PART AUTOBIOGRAPHY AND PUBLISHED BY MERCAT PRESS.

Jess Smith's mother and Uncle Charlie

Ivy Lee

Clockwise from top — Mary Lee; Gypsy Encampment; Some of the Price family by the River Linnet at Bury St Edmunds just before WW2

Top — Mary Lee;
bottom — Bill Price and wife

Clockwise from top left — Jim Lee; La La Lee;
Suzie Lee and her brother

Top — Florrie Lee and family;
bottom — Little Di and friend

Both photos:
Florrie Lee

Top A Gypsy family;
bottom — Gypsy father with his baby

*Clockwise from top — Fred and Creddy Lee; Reuben Lee and Winky Price
Righteous Price*

Elizabeth Price

*Top left — Gypsy child; right — Gypsy boy;
bottom — Lina, Blondy, Mother and Cooly Price*

Top — Old Naily Lee;
bottom — Hope Price, Jack Price, John Taylor, Dadda Price, Young Price,
Gypsy Boy Price and Pretty Boy Price

La La and Ivy Lee on their wedding day

Loma and Pora Lee

Top — Fred and John Lee;
bottom — Blackie Lee

Top Photo includes Deer, Puppy, Sister and Hopie Lee;
bottom photo includes Olivine, Carol and Linda

A fine old varda

Melinda Price with daughter Lucy Price

Linchum Smith and his daughter

Top — Ron Lee, Linchum Smith; Monty, Andy, Cocky and Ivor Lee, and friends;
bottom — Young Gypsy children with their horse

*Left — Andy Riley, brother of Dilly Riley who married Jack Price;
right — Hope, Peter, Lizzy, Jack and Beryl Boggy Price*

Left — A beautiful young Gypsy woman, Beryl Lena Price, then aged 19, with her younger sister Martina, taken at Newark;
right — Beryl Lena Price, aged 3, daughter of Jack and Dilly Price on the front of a wagon

Top — The Burton family, The boy on the horse is Old Noah, son of Data Burton. Also on the picture is Hughie Burton, known as Big Jess; bottom — Maggie Evans, wife of Crimea Price

Top — Jack Price and his daughter Beryl Lena, chatting to his cousin, also Jack Price;
bottom — A step back in time to the days of clothes peg making. Brothers Crimea and Jack Price with children Andy, John, Beryl Lena and Minty.

Skegness days: Top — John Price and his nephew Nipper;
bottom — John Price and his cousin Winky Price

Top — Sam Price-Hawkins on Skegness Beach;
bottom — The Price family including, in the background, Jack Price, and
at the front his four sons Sam, Andy, John and Creddy (known as Tich)

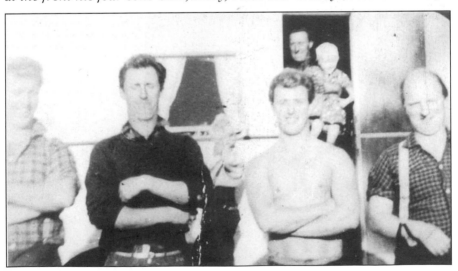

Bunny Price and friend

Beryl Lena Burton, granddaughter of Wit Wat Burton and Beryl Lena;
great granddaughter of Jack and Dilly Price and Noah and Sophie Burton

The Born Again Movement

The born again Christian movement began in the USA in the 1950s and was initiated mainly by T.L. Osborne, an evangelical Baptist preacher. It quickly spread to France and especially Brittany where Rev Clement Le Cossac led the evangelical Pentecostal mission, "Light and Life".

Gypsy preachers and pastors began coming to Britain and started converting Gypsies to evangelical Christianity. Now, in Britain, over half of all Britain's Traditional Travellers are thought to be connected to the movement and the movement has had a profound effect. Not least, heavy drinking that was a feature of the lives of some Travellers because of the hardship and despair they faced, is far less of a problem than ever, and crime and antisocial behavior are frowned upon.

Though some people claim that the culture has been adversely affected, others deny this and see the benefits that the movement has brought. All over Britain, people have begun to study the Bible and become pastors themselves, preaching to their own people. Some have attended Bible College in the USA to increase their knowledge and understanding. Several Light and Life churches now exist in various parts of the UK.
The Himley Hall convention — between Wolverhampton and Dudley — shown in the following photos, was one of the first to be held and one of the biggest ever. It took place in August 1984 and 150 men and women were baptised in the name of Jesus and the Father and the Holy Ghost. The organisers were Clifford Lee, Bill Price, Raymond Clee, Fred Price and Dai Lee.

Top — John Price, man of God, and his daughter;
bottom — Harry Watton being baptised by (left) Leonard Price) and (right)
Bill Price, who was an organizer of the Light and Life convention.

145

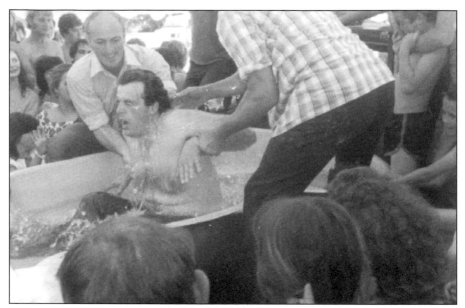

Top — Scoby Price, one of many men and women to be baptized; bottom — Raymond Clee (with beard and white shirt), one of the organisers of the convention

*Top — Dai Lee at Himley Hall Convention, also a Convention organizer;
bottom — a meeting at the same convention with children Amand and
Julie Price*

Top — women at the Himley Hall Convention;
bottom — cooking on a barbecue.

Bottom, Peggy Lee, wife of Lavern

John Price and his dog

Top — Winky Price, Old Billy Price and Lina; bottom — Bill Price and Rudy Price

Top — A happy day out.
bottom, Old La La Lee.

 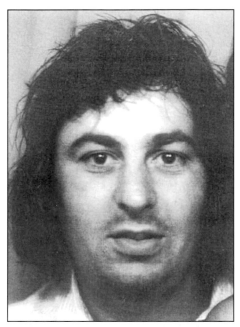

Clockwise from top left - Ivy Lee, Blackie; bottom, two pictures of Old La La

Clockwise from top left — Gypsy children having a picnic, La La lee's wife, a child at play.

Emily Slender who was mother of Nelly, Data, Darkess, Lucy and Polly, along with Casey Price and children Ivy and Emily.

Left — Thorney; right — Linchum's sister

Left — Chasey Price and children;
right — Andy and Darkess Smith.

About 1938 — stopping on a piece of ground at Bury St Edmunds, near the river Linnet. The land belonged to Lady Macraw, a traditional Price and Lee stopping ground for more years than anyone can remember. Shown here are , front, left to right, Othie Lee (uncle of William) with his sons baby Clifford, Shaun and Othie (the eldest). At the back — Julie Lee, Lena Price, Samson Price. Lena Price (mother of William), Beryl Price and William Price (senior — William's father).

Ivor and Rosanna Price

Carol, Fred, Deer and Chassey Lee with Baby Fred Price and Chassey Price

Top — Tommy and Esther Lee with Raynor, Viner, Mollie and others;
bottom — Loma, Rosie, Debbie and Marty Lee with their children.

Crystal Price, the author's daughter